Why Are You Smiling?

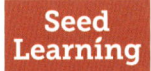

smiling

crying

frowning

yawning

coughing

laughing

sighing

blushing

Why are you smiling?

Because I'm happy.

Why are you crying?

Because I'm sad.

Why are you frowning?

Because I'm angry.

Why are you coughing?

Because I'm sick.

Why are you sighing?

Because I'm bored.

Why are you yawning?

Because I'm tired.

Let's learn about Thailand.

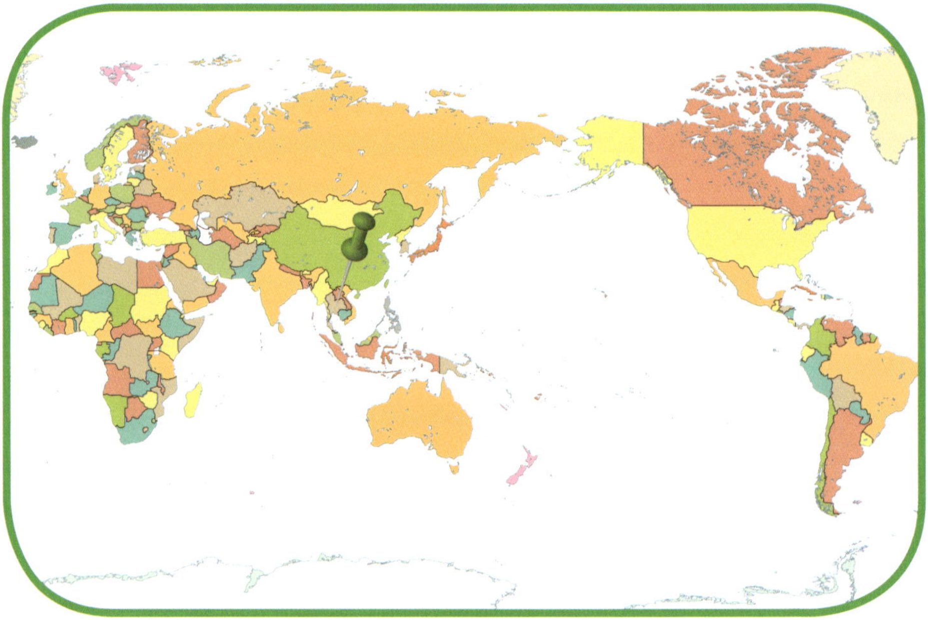

Flag of Thailand

Floating market